All Abou

Contents

written by Julie Ellis

obsidian

Glass has been used for a long time. The first glass came from a volcano. The fire inside the volcano was so hot that it made sand melt.

When the sand got cold again, it had turned into glass. This glass is called obsidian. A long time ago, people used it as a tool.

Glass is made by heating sand
with some other things.
The sand melts in the hot fire.

4

When the melted sand gets cold, it is glass. A lot of glass is used for doors or windows.

windows

Glass can be made in pretty colors.
Other things are added to the sand
to make it turn different colors.

Gold, silver, and copper can be used.
Glass can be made blue, red, green,
yellow, or any other color.

A glassblower blows through a tube into hot glass to make shapes.

The glass stays in this new shape when it gets cold. This is how vases and other pretty things are made.

Some people like making new things out of pieces of colored glass.

warm glass work

They can melt pieces of glass together to make bright beads. This is called warm glass work.

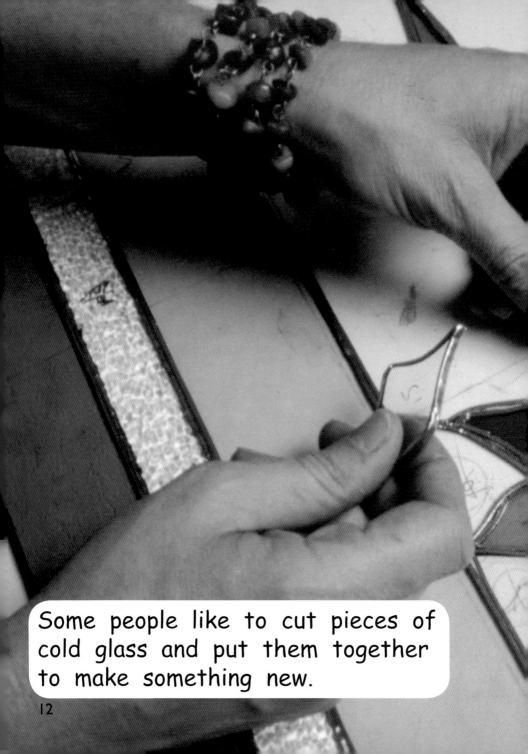

Some people like to cut pieces of cold glass and put them together to make something new.

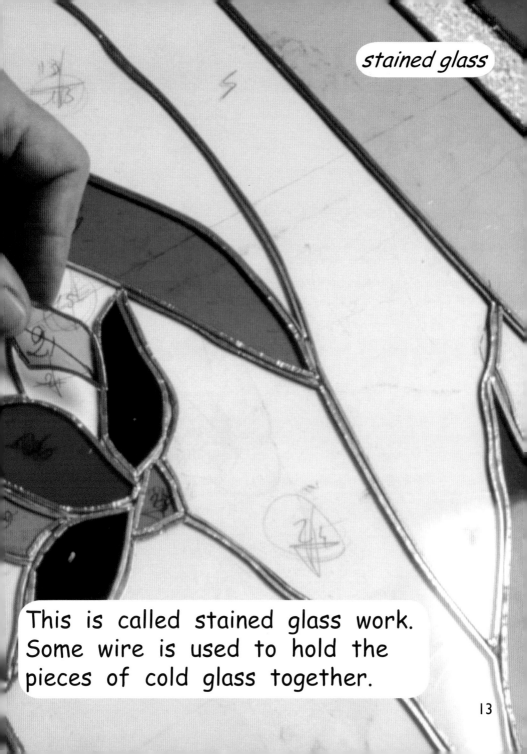

stained glass

This is called stained glass work. Some wire is used to hold the pieces of cold glass together.

GL
CLEAR, GR
NO YELLOW,
REMOVE L

GLASS

GLASS

Old glass can be used again and again. Our old jars and bottles can be put into bins to go to the factory.

ASS

, & BROWN ONLY
UE, OR BLACK GLASS
S & RINSE CLEAN

Then the glass is broken up and
melted to make new things.
This work is called recycling.

Many things are made from glass. Can you tell which things were made from hot glass, warm glass, cold glass, or old glass?